YOUR SOUL IS REQUIRED

Truth of the Unending Self

Katrece Howard

Words of Understanding
Publishers LLC

Words of Understanding Publishing © 2021

ISBN: 978-0-9881830-6-3

This book is dedicated to the Byers Family
who in love and friendship have always been
a source of strength to our family.

CONTENTS

INTRODUCTION

"But God said to him, 'Fool! This night **your soul will be required** of you; then whose will those things be which you have provided?' So is he who lays up treasure for himself, and is not rich toward God" (Luke 12:20-21).

N ervously finding the room of the unfamiliar college, I sit down waiting for the execution. No one speaks as the clock ticks down while we all hold number two pencils. If there is any means to jettison me from that moment in time I will gratefully go. But I stay and answer the questions as best I can by filling in bubbles on the page in hopeful despair. To enter higher learning after high school I must take one of the college board exams. The university cares not of my apprehension of taking a standardized test. I must comply and receive a certain score to be considered for their program. It is required.

What is required of you? Paying taxes, driving on the right side of the road, or wearing clothes in public are just a few duties we expect ourselves and others to adhere. While some look for loopholes in any given task out of slothfulness or distain, the majority do what is asked. We submit income tax, obey driving laws, and don appropriate clothes to go out. People do what is required out of necessity, for ease in a situation or to avoid unwanted consequences. However, there are much weightier matters so many ignore in life. What of spiritual requirements that possess an eternal answer?

The passage in Luke refers to a rich man with a great harvest who knows only the pronoun "I." No consideration for others in the bounty just acquired, no sharing with neighbors in need, no looking to feed family and friends, he thinks solely of his enrichment and continued wealth. Surely Charles Dickens thought of this Bible passage as he penned the character Scrooge in A Christmas Carol. But centuries earlier Jesus taught in the parable where our priority should be. Unlike the Dickens tale, the Bible lesson does not have the same happy ending. God tells the man his soul is required that night and it is too late to change the outcome. It is not too late for you the reader. Paramount in writing this work becomes the need to guide you to the most essential book, the Bible, and show its teaching of the essential part of you. This study teaches the truth of our souls from the biblical text. Let us learn the simplicity of the Word, the logic of His commands, and the reward of listening to our Creator. Do you understand the soul God speaks of? Are you ready to answer if the question were asked of you?

CHAPTER ONE: A SOUL DEFINED

Descending the stairs, she glanced in horror as the young man sitting on the living room couch casually opened her father's can of mixed nuts scooping a handful and the contents disappearing before she could enter the room. He was oblivious to the unwritten law of leaving Daddy's can of nuts alone. It was reserved for watching Saturday football of his alma mater Clemson. She excused the behavior as nerves on a first date. She hastily whisked him out the door, teaching him how to dodge the spiderwebs in the wooded yard of her home. His boyish face and silly manner erased the crime executed before her eyes. After all, he did play the bagpipe, wear obscure t-shirts, and most shocking, occasionally listened to polka. What did she see in him? This man was polar opposite any person in her sphere. He laughed boisterously; she was quiet. He rambled about topics unheard of; she listened patiently. He labored with an artist using his innate talent; she was still finding her artistic ability. But he in gentleness, intelligence, and humor proved his worth. He had the worth from the beginning; she needed to rethink her world.

Initially my parents were guarded and confused as to this oddity that wandered into a daughter's life and thrust into theirs. In their minds there could not have been a greater mismatch if Daffy Duck had shown up instead. To my parents William was not made to order and were certain no one ordered him at all. To them he was a character who shows up as a comedic complication to a sitcom family on TV. They were now that sitcom family and were unsure what to think.

William was born in a part of Mississippi where every other house displays three rusted cars in the front yard as lawn ornaments. I was born and reared in Florida, lived in the shade of live oaks and St. Augustine grass with an overly reserved family in speech and manner. We both were the youngest of three siblings, loved vintage Looney Tunes, and possessed some drawing and painting supplies. Besides the outside interests in common, we each foremost believed in our Creator, obeyed His word, and patterned our lives by God's precepts.

I am sure my mother's parents considered my father just as strange when he suddenly arrived at their house (though my Daddy was never Daffy). My parents wondered why William was the way he was. He did not fit any customary category they could imagine. They did not mind uniqueness as a quality, but this? Here lies the unpredictability in it all. He was unique, but so too was their daughter. Here resides both the certainty and the mystery inside each person – the human soul. My husband and I are two souls. Independent from each other yet joined. Two souls come together to be one in marriage. Why are we the way we are? The "we" in this question includes all humanity. It is the soul within. We are affected by environment. That is true. But we are not the embodiment of our environment. We are affected by chemistry in our bodies and our bodies also. That is true. But character is not the sum total of chemicals or the body's narrow limitations. There is someone at the core of our being. It is the true self. Each of us is a singular and extraordinary creation by God. He designs a stand-alone individual. God does not use a cookie cutter approach. One soul is not exactly like all others. This soul will have a name, not as a matter of practicality but as a designation of individuality and personhood. This soul will have a personality that cannot be entirely explained by environment or chemistry or anything material. Behaviors, reactions, temperament, disposition, and feelings can all be shaped and reshaped through time, experience, and maturity. But there is a subject which must preexist to be affected by time, experience, and maturity. That subject displays immediate selfhood. Parents who have more than one child know very soon that each infant is different from the last. This is a new person with his or her own distinctions. This is someone, not something. Swaddled and in diapers is a soul beginning everything.

My husband and I are soulmates laboring here on earth looking forward to a heavenly home. We have learned each other's personality, and that is dealing with the soul within. To love the soul is to truly love the person. It is to love who they are and what they are. It is to love them beyond what is convenient or what is physical. To love the soul is to know that part of them is eternal. It is to know they will exist somewhere after billions of years. It is to want the best for them beyond this life on earth.

Often in the obituaries one finds long columns written of the person deceased. Listed are the family members left behind and those who preceded the death. It tells of their career and accomplishments, what organizations they affiliated, and to what religion they belonged. Perhaps it mentions what a loving spouse, grandparent, and sibling they were to the family. These are comforting words to read. Though much can be said of one's life to show respect at their passing, they are temporary thoughts. What should be stated of a life to convey importance?

For what is your life? It is even a vapor that appears for a little time and then vanishes away (James 4:14).

Above all, if the reader takes nothing else, the one lasting fact to remember: life evaporates but is not the end. Even those blessed with many years can still be compared as a candle blown out. James reminds man, by his illustration, life vanishes like the wisping vapor never to be seen again on earth. But each life will continue. While I do not claim to be a great scholar, perfect individual, or engaging, witty author, I do have a burning desire to share in a clear, well-thought manner the truth of the soul's eternity. There are times in any home when a lite cleaning will not do – surface wiping is not enough. It takes a greater effort for a deep cleaning in order to get the house in its best condition. The same idea applies to a casual reading of a subject or truly comprehending and exhaustively covering the whole matter. Hence, this book is written to help the reader to grasp the scriptural truth, to convey the urgency of believing the Bible, and attest the fact that all souls continue to another realm.

The Bible remains the one essential tool in anyone's hand. Though maligned and ignored it is only in this book we learn doctrine, reproof, correction, and instruction in righteousness (2 Timothy 3:16-17) to have a well-lived life and a soul continuing to a rich reward. Several men and women in the Bible have summations of their lives and the words are few. Enoch **walked with God** (Genesis 5:22). It is extraordinary that someone who lived 365 years, had sons and daughters, and was a prophet (Jude 1:14-15) has his life summed up with three words: "walked with God." That truly is an economy of words. Though brief, those three words speak volumes. There is no way to know what Enoch faced in his life – the challenges, the successes, the loss, the sleepless nights, or the persecutions. He must have been a great man and certainly far greater even than those who were called **mighty men who *were* of old, men of renown,** or even **men of valor.** The others did amazing things on the earth but their works ended and any trace of their names and deeds quickly vanished. Whatever they did could not last nor was it enough to be taken by God to now reside with Him (Genesis 5:24).

Three times God called Job **blameless and upright** (Job 1:1, 8; 2:3). On two occasions Paul described Tychicus as **a beloved brother and faithful minister in the Lord** (Ephesians 6:21; Colossians 4:7). The apostle John said **Demetrius has a good testimony from all** (3 John 1:12). Abigail **was a woman of good understanding** (1 Samuel 25:3). Anna **did not depart from the temple, but served God with fastings and prayers night and day** (Luke 2:37). Joseph was called a **just man** (Matthew 1:19). In Acts 10:2, Cornelius was described as **a devout *man* and one who feared God with all his household.** Simeon **was just and devout** (Luke 2:25). Jesus summed up Nathanael when he said, **"Behold, an Israelite indeed, in whom is no deceit!"** (John 1:47). In Genesis 6:9, Noah was called a **just man, perfect in his generations.** Moses was called **the ser-**

vant of the Lord (Joshua 1:13).

God can also describe entire groups in the same way. In 1 Kings 19:18 and Romans 11:4, God described a group of **seven thousand in Israel, all whose knees have not bowed to Baal.** In the book of Revelation, an elder speaking to John described another group: **These are the ones who come out of the great tribulation, and washed their robes and made them white in the blood of the Lamb** (Revelation 7:14).

The carefully chosen words speak volumes of the life they lived. What few words should you hope to have stated on your behalf? *He was a servant of God. She was a faithful Christian.* What more needs to be said? A faithful servant will incorporate righteousness in all parts of her life without long addresses. He will have been the obedient child, the devoted spouse, the caring parent, and dedicated worker for the Lord. Not perfect but mercifully saved by God's grace. Though the newspaper obituary may state a hometown and age in parting words, the destination of that soul is the import. If it cannot be said that you "walked with God", nothing else matters.

In early memories most of us loved and trusted our parents. They were our tender caregivers and the first faces we observed. We believed them to be our entire world though at the time our world was somewhat limited. Most of us obeyed what we were asked, followed where they led, and abided by their rules. As children grow older, they begin to question what has been taught, not always out of rebellion but as an outcome of developing as a separate being. They are becoming independent in mind and their own person. This is normal. Every individual should give great thought to what is happening in life, where they fit and why they exist. In today's world with fast internet and instant meals, pondering serious issues does not enter some minds. A minority may consider spiritual weighty matters briefly to then return to what is at hand. A Bible-believing person comes to a firm conclusion and steps forward in fulfilling his role. But one who has no spiritual foundation falters. The majority lose interest in the matter concluding there is no answer, or they think man's ideas are perfect enough and thus will not listen to their Creator.

> **The fear of the Lord is the beginning of knowledge, But fools despise wisdom and instruction** (Proverbs 1:7).

Why would a fool despise wisdom and instruction? Because he denies his need for a greater truth. He cannot be bothered. His thoughts are on the here and now to fill his immediate want. A fool puts no effort to think beyond today but only looks down to his limited sphere. This creates the fool. However, those who want godly knowledge will look above the earthly life for heavenly guidance. **"Fear of the Lord"** in Proverbs chapter one speaks of respect and awe of God's power along with the fear of repercussion for wrong. Punishment has always been a great motivator in my life. A glance from one of my parents in disapproval was enough. A spanking was a dark cloud over my head in sickening guilt and a sore seat. They were devoted parents who believed correction comes from love. Some children develop a careless attitude, feeling free to do as they please with no fear of getting in trouble. But I was the opposite. Even as an adult I go to great lengths to please those around me and not be thought of as difficult.

So that same wiring in my being increased as I studied the Bible and learned how each soul is accountable to God. Simply put, I do not want to go to Hell and do not wish that reality on any. Often I try to visualize what that existence would be, but it cannot compare with the very real permanence of Hell. And with that determination I strive to help others to see the truth of God's word so they will understand. That is the determination in which I write this book. What is the point of this life if one does not believe outside of his everyday existence? Surely, feelings of hopelessness and continuing disbelief fuel the rate of suicide in our land. While some people have a vague concept of life after death, others do not dare think beyond today. Much has been written on philosophy, mythology, and psychology, but the majority is misinformation which helps no one. Emphasis in education from kindergarten to college focuses on learning all subjects and books published excluding the Bible. But only the Bible teaches the truth of an eternal place where our souls will continue. That is a truth each soul must know. Conversely, I also need to help others learn of God's outpouring of love for each soul, not just the punishment and justice for sinfulness. There is a balance in the justice of God understood in His word.

Let us define the word *soul*. Webster defines soul as "the immaterial essence, animating principle, or actuating cause of an individual life. The spiritual principle embodied in human beings."(merriam-webster.com). Here is the age-old understanding of the dichotomy of man. There are two sides to each of us. The body is the physical side, the earthly and biological. The soul is the spiritual side. It is eternal. While our earthly side will come to an end, our spiritual side will never end. Easily understood, the body is comprised of material flesh which can be seen and felt. Nevertheless, humans have a spiritual part given by their Creator which has certain unique attributes. Just as real as one's five senses of sight, smell, hearing, touch, and taste, the soul is even more vital. Man learns to live if denied one of the senses. However, the soul, though not as easily detected, cannot be dismissed. The word *soul* in the Old Testament is rendered *nephesh* from the Hebrew meaning "a breathing creature." Considering the context, it can refer to the physical person or the spiritual part of an individual. In Isaiah 55:2, "soul" refers to basic physical necessity, while conversely in Psalm 19:7, "soul" is used to speak of the spiritual.

Listen carefully to Me, and eat what is good,
And let your soul delight itself in abundance.
Isaiah 55:2

The law of the Lord is perfect, converting the soul;

Psalm 19:7

* * *

The Lord is my shepherd; I shall not want.
He makes me lie down in green pastures;
He leads me beside still waters.
He restores my soul;
He leads me in the paths of righteousness
For His name's sake.
Psalm 23:1-3

Psalm twenty-three records a recognized set of verses with some having it memorized. We tend to hear it recited during funerals or printed on cards of encouragement. The author, David, uses the words to reflect peace in his daily walk. But we all find benefit in the thoughts. God restores my soul. What does this mean? His love compels me to continue. He guides me to find rest, shows me the right way in His word, and cares for me as His creation. Comfort comes from these words in Psalm with visual imagery of His love. Jesus in the New Testament teaches us with comforting words in Matthew 5:1-12 regarding blessings the followers of God can receive, commonly referred as the Beatitudes. Our souls will benefit by living close to the precepts given in the Bible. Mankind thrives and exists fulfilled by obeying God.

Beloved, I pray that you may prosper in all things and be in health, just as your soul prospers (3 John 2).

Are you a soul who denies a Creator? This book is for you. Are you a Bible believer but actually leans on men's doctrine or denominational teaching not found in the Bible? This book is for you. Are you a Christian who diligently meditates on God's word but have not considered the scope of the soul and how it differs and relates to the body? This book is for you. In this study the secular definition is given, vast amounts of related scriptures shared, and simple logic presented to help the reader grasp the subject of the soul.

CHAPTER TWO: WHO GAVE US A SOUL?

How much fun can it be to roll a rubber ball back and forth down a long hallway? Enough pleasure to occupy me and my sister for hours. The bedroom doors would be shut, but the trick was not to let the ball escape down the stairs. During the Olympic rubber ball event (most are unaware of its existence), we would talk, laugh, and bond. Heavy debate ensued as to who was the superior character from the Banana Splits (a Saturday morning TV show), which Beatle wrote better songs, and which of us possessed the greater Hot Wheels collection. As older girls we sequestered in a bedroom listening to albums, singing along in harmony. She was soprano; I was alto. We are close sisters and I view our relationship as one in the Bible: **"the soul of Jonathan was knit to the soul of David, and Jonathan loved him as his own soul"** (1 Samuel 18:1). She patiently comforted me after bad dreams, played evening badminton until we could not see the birdy in the dark, and lovingly called me Kitty Kat. I see the same closeness in our two sons, though different in temperament, akin in interest, humor, and devotion. A soul can connect to another in earthly relationships, but our connection with God is paramount.

It is easier to ignore than obey. That truth is man's downfall. Many dismiss the Bible as another book written by men and its contents carry no information worthwhile. How can we know for certain the words are given by a superior mind who created us? We close our ears. As a young girl, I could upset my friend by stopping my ears to anything she was telling me. A childish defiance works to get a six-year-old from listening to another, but is not quite as effective as one grows into an adult. And adults can be just as defiant. By relying on the inability to answer important questions of life, most justify giving spiritual matters no more thought. It is simply put down as something we cannot know and therefore is of no concern. But should we not be sure of these weighty subjects when an eternal outcome is dependent on them? All questions are answered by God's word which each person must consider. Now that we discussed the soul from a biblical and secular definition, a logical question follows. Who gave us a soul?

Genesis chapter one, the first chapter of the first book of the Bible, begins by teaching us how everything we see and beyond what we can see was formed. Creation must have been truly awesome if one could have witnessed any part. But we must rely on the words given in the text and the beauty seen around us to appreciate the world was designed by a perfect designer.

The earth was without form, and void; and darkness was on the face of the deep. And the Spirit of God was hovering over the face of the waters. Then God said, "Let there be light"; and there was light. And God saw the light, that it was good; and God divided the light from the darkness. God called the light Day, and the darkness He called Night (Genesis 1:2-5).

God is eternal. He is from everlasting to everlasting. **Before the mountains were brought forth, Or ever You had formed the earth and the world, Even from everlasting to everlasting, You are God** (Psalm 90:2). In Genesis 1:2-5, light contrasts darkness with God giving the names day and night. This first dividing of light and darkness was day one and all days have counted from then.

Then God said, "Let there be a firmament in the midst of the waters, and let it divide the waters from the waters" (Genesis 1:6).

God separates waters calling it the firmament, heaven, on day two. Firmament is defined as the expanse of air surrounding the earth. Man observes it as the magnificent sky. Water is placed above and below the firmament. In time the water above the firmament came crashing back to the earth in the days of Noah when **"the windows of heaven were opened"** (Genesis 7:11).

> **And God called the dry land Earth, and the gathering together of the waters He called Seas. And God saw that it was good** (Genesis 1:10).

On day three land and sea are separated. The dry land is called Earth and the first plants emerge. The creation of plants is the beginning of life on earth. Every grass, herb, and tree are commanded to yield seed and fruit after its kind- a law set in nature witnessed every year through the centuries. The beauty and power displayed in the very concept of land, plants, and seas is ample evidence of a powerful and intelligent designer. The world was made robust and capable of sustaining life from the third day of creation to today. How is that possible? A constant supply of food, water, and air are only a small part of what was brought together on day three. These continue to work as they were designed to do from the start. Man is only beginning to understand the many facets and functions of how these sustain the earth.

> **Then God said, "Let there be lights in the firmament of the heavens to divide the day from the night; and let them be for signs and seasons, and for days and years; and let them be for lights in the firmament of the heavens to give light on the earth"; and it was so** (Genesis 1:14-15).

Two great lights are created by God on day four. The sun is the greater light ruling the day and the moon is the lesser light ruling the night. Planets and stars are perfectly placed in the outer reaches to give signs and seasons to Creation. Beside the splendor of the skies, all these are designed to show the passing of time. The lights created divide day and night. All of it is regular and predictable. Sunrise is the beginning of the day and sundown marks the beginning of night. The phases of the moon display the passing of time inside a month. The stars show the passing of seasons and years. The sky is a magnificent clock and calendar which ancient and modern man use as a matter of course. As is often the case in the creation of God, many things serve multiple purposes. Sunlight also benefits the plant life created the day before and everything that will be created on the next two days.

> **Then God said, "Let the waters abound with an abundance of living creatures, and let birds fly above the earth across the face of the firmament of the heavens"** (Genesis 1:20).

On day five, marine life flourishes in the oceans. The words **abound with an abundance** gives the extent to God's creativity. He did no meager job. He created. From surface to vast depths, the oceans are full of life. To this day the waters are teaming with life from the microscopic to the immense, bacteria to whales. In places where man was certain no life could possibly exist there is life as God created it on day five. On the same day, God formed all the flying creatures. Birds fill the skies and make their nests in the trees and dry ground. Their Creator commands them all to be fruitful and multiply and fill the seas and sky.

> **Then God said, "Let the earth bring forth the living creature according to its kind: cattle and creeping thing and beast of the earth, each according to its kind"; and it was so** (Genesis 1:24).

> **Then God said, "Let Us make man in Our image, according to Our likeness; let them have dominion over the fish of the sea, over the birds of the air, and over the cattle, over all the earth and over every creeping thing that creeps on the earth." So God created man in His own image; in the image of God He created him; male and female He created them"** (Genesis 1:26-27).

On the sixth day, God creates all land animals according to

its kind on the earth. This would include what centuries later are named dinosaurs. No evolutionary morphing from one creature into another; every kind of land creature was formed on this day. In the final part of God's plan, man is created in His image with the command to have dominion over fish, birds, cattle, and every creeping thing on the earth. Man is designed to have dominion over all creation as God commanded. Everything was created with mankind in mind. Nothing in creation has a greater importance than man. Man is created last since everything in creation is meant to serve mankind. Nothing has a greater importance or need than mankind, not animals, not trees, not the earth itself. The idea of everything being destroyed by climate change is to remove God from His creation. It comes from atheism. The idea of animals having greater rights than people is to move the love of God from man to animals. They are created for man's use. These creatures will eventually come to an end. Mankind is eternal.

Each massive creation is but spoken into existence each day by our omnipotent God. The seventh day, the Creation ends with God stating all was very good (Genesis 1:31). He blessed and sanctified day seven because He rested (ceased) from all His work.

All we come to comprehend begins in those first seven days resulting in our week. Our Creator tells us all we need in precise words which are recorded for us to understand, to refer, and to teach. God proclaims His supremacy in the book of Isaiah: **For thus says the Lord, Who created the heavens, Who is God, Who formed the earth and made it, Who has established it, Who did not create it in vain, Who formed it to be inhabited: "I am the Lord, and there is no other"** (Isaiah 45:18).

For the Beauty of the Earth, a hymn written by Folliott S. Pierpoint (1835-1917), conveys his love of God, gratitude for His blessings, and wonder at the creation viewed around him.

For the beauty of the earth, For the glory of the skies,
For the love which from our birth Over and around us lies.

For the joy of human love, Brother, sister, parent, child,
Friends on earth, and friends above, For all gentle tho'ts and mild.
For Thy church that evermore Lifteth holy hands above,
Offering up on every shore Her pure sacrifice of love,
Lord of all, to Thee we raise
This our hymn of grateful praise.

And the Lord God formed man of the dust of the ground, and breathed into his nostrils the breath of life; and man became a living soul (Genesis 2:7 KJV).

Who gave us a soul? Genesis clearly answers, "God." The New King James Version renders Genesis 2:7 as **"and man became a living being."** The King James Version, previously quoted, translated the same verse as **"and man became a living soul."** Both translations accurately refer to the Hebrew word *nephesh*. In one perfectly crafted sentence, the details of the creation of the first man and his soul are given. God forms Adam (the man) from the dust of the ground and then forms woman from Adam's rib (Genesis 2:22). She is given the name *Eve* meaning "the mother of all living." These two created beings begin with a soul, and children born after are also souls, though the creation man stands alone and above the rest. He remains the final work unique from animals, earth and universe. Man is created in the image of God and is an eternal being. Once the soul is bestowed it will not cease when the body ceases but will be taken to another existence.

No scripture in the Bible explains visually how the image of God looks. Man cannot look at God to observe His form. We must take God at His word and be content with the knowledge given. One truth is certain – man has not evolved from apes or any creature over vast amounts of time, or out of amoeba in a puddle of slime. Those lies are concocted to explain man's existence without a Creator. The truth is in the Bible with the origin of man given in certainty. Clearly man reigns superior to the rest of creation with the command to have dominion over the creatures. Placed in a perfect garden with the instruction to tend and keep it, Adam has everything. However, God did not want man to be alone thus provided the perfect helper to him – woman. "**And Adam said: 'This is now bone of my bones And flesh of my flesh; She shall be called Woman, Because she was taken out of Man'**" (Genesis 2:23). Adam and Eve are then commanded to **"be fruitful and multiply; fill the earth and subdue it"** (Genesis 1:28).

Into this perfect world enters the villain. Satan, in the form of a serpent, speaks to Eve to question the authority and motive of God. By only adding the word "not" into one of the commands, he tempts Eve to sin and, by implication, calls God a liar (Genesis 3:4). She listens to Satan instead of her Creator. Adam joins her in the sin as both bring sin into a perfect world, causing spiritual death for their souls and the remainder of their life in hardship. In vain, both try to hide from God and cover their bodies in what they now see as shame. Their Maker lovingly questions both though He fully knows what has occurred. However, their sin has consequences. God drives them out of the garden after pronouncing punishment to each including the serpent (Genesis 3:14-19). Satan becomes the tempter to every soul born. Revelation 12:9 teaches **"that serpent of old, called the Devil and Satan, … deceives the whole world."** We are warned by Peter, **"Be sober, be vigilant; because your adversary the devil walks about like a roaring lion, seeking whom he may devour"** (1 Peter 5:8). The description Peter gives should terrify us. Once a lion has a meal in sight, he hunts stealthily using all his power for the kill. Satan, full of hate, preys on every soul, craving their destruction. Satan even came to Jesus (Matthew 4:1-11) to tempt Him with the same sins he uses on mankind. But our Lord overcame the Tempter replying with scripture and commanding him to leave. His example inspires us to remain deaf to Satan's temptations. Reassurance comes as we read, **"Resist the devil and he will flee from you"** (James 4:7). Those inspired words let me know I can overcome temptation with good (Romans 12:21).

God bestowed a precious gift to each with a soul. Often

when you receive a gift you feel the desire to return the kindness. How much more a gift from God? Our relationship with our Creator must be foremost in our minds. I separate myself from God by sin and need redemption for the saving of my soul. Jesus Christ is our Savior (Luke 2:11) and Redeemer (Isaiah 44:6). God, in giving us our soul, looks to receive us back to Him at our obedience.

CHAPTER THREE: THE DISTINCTION
BETWEEN BODY AND SOUL

O nce morning sickness subsided for each of my three preg-
nancies, William and I began singing to our children while
each developed in the womb. He would sing the alphabet, books
of the Bible, and Nat King Cole standards to my burgeoning
middle before we saw that child emerge. It was not to fast-track
learning to great future achievements but to let the child know
he or she was loved and anticipated. We steadfastly affirm, before birth, a soul grows inside the mother and needs care from the
start. That soul was part of us, had a name, and was loved before
we saw his or her face.

As defined in chapter one *soul* refers to the spiritual essence
of each human being. In numerous passages in the Bible the word
soul links with the heart, mind, and strength when speaking of
man's spiritual condition. God instructs the Israelites in Deuteronomy 6:5, **"You shall love the Lord your God with all your heart,
with all your soul, and with all your strength."** In Matthew 22:37
when a lawyer questioned our Lord, **Jesus said to him, "You shall
love the Lord your God with all your heart, with all your soul,
and with all your mind."** Both scriptures taken together create
a list incorporating heart, soul, strength, and mind. This means
the whole of your being is unified in one purpose – the love of
God. This is not to be taken as body or biology only. The literal
organ of the human heart is incapable of any emotion or loyalty.
The strength of our bodies is also incapable of understanding
love. Mind and soul, however, are fully capable of comprehending
and expressing all possible emotions and attitudes: love and al-
legiance, abhorrence and betrayal. These control the outpouring
of all strength and effort toward what we love. Though the word
heart is used as the seat of emotion, it is the mind and the soul
where devotion and the will to love are found. These scriptures

view our whole person or being as dedicated to God. These are distinct points between the body and the soul which need to be understood.

First, let us consider the physical body. At the point of conception, we are of material substance beginning to grow inside the womb. While inside this environment, the process continues of developing body structures. Physical life has begun.

> **For You formed my inward parts; You covered me in my mother's womb. I will praise You, for I am fearfully and wonderfully made; Marvelous are Your works, And that my soul knows very well** (Psalm 139:13-14).

The moment conception occurs, there is human life. Human life begins before birth not at birth as argued and legislated by man's court. God gave man the law to regard and obey.

> **Whoever sheds man's blood, By man his blood shall be shed; For in the image of God He made man** (Genesis 9:6).

Stated again in Genesis remains the fact that man is in the image of God. Logically, every person is protected by God since every person is made in His image. This would include any age (young or old) or ability (useful or impaired). Thus, abortion and euthanasia are the murder of innocent human life. We do not need a ruling or opinion from man – God made this ruling from the beginning and established His law. There is nothing man may do to change this. By man's law excusing and allowing this crime, he is guilty of murder. It is listed among the seven things the Lord hates: **"Hands that shed innocent blood"** (Proverbs 6:17).

Our Maker designed us with intricate systems of the body: cardiovascular, digestive, endocrine, excretory, immune, integu-

mentary, musculoskeletal, nervous, respiratory, and reproduct-
ive. These are named and categorized by man but formed by
God. Each system works in conjunction with and is dependent
on the others to provide a stable and healthy body which can be
called *homeostasis*. In His design, man can eat food, derive the
needed nutrients, satisfy hunger, and eliminate the waste. Man
can breathe in oxygen to live and exhale carbon dioxide. Blood
can be pumped throughout the body by the beating heart. Skin
can receive a cut and heal itself. The human body in its astound-
ing structure shouts it is shaped by an awesome force. *Awesome*
becomes a word said frivolously to describe anything from new
sneakers to the latest music. It cannot be said of everything, **"for
the Lord your God is God of gods and Lord of lords, the great
God, mighty and awesome"** (Deuteronomy 10:17). With all the
evidence of design, the body could not logically be made without
a Designer. Chance generates nothing but a chaotic mess. Inside
each named system, separate parts of the body display complex-
ity. Man acknowledges the wisdom in these parts using them as
a pattern for engineering inventions such as the camera (eye),
mechanical arm for assembly work (arm), and artificial intelligence (brain). Though he may not attribute the blueprint from
God, man understands the brilliance therein.

God demonstrates His love for man in His care for his physical body. He clothed man and woman (Genesis 3:21), incorporating what God sees as modest apparel. In Genesis 3, the coats God
made for Adam and Eve covered them from the shoulder to knee.
Not only for protection of skin but covering what our Creator
deems as nakedness. The world's opinion of modest clothing is
unimportant if we are to please God. Obeying His word guards us
from lustful thoughts and acts. Commanded more than in the Old
Testament, this can be understood from 1 Peter 2:11: **"abstain
from fleshly lust which war against the soul."** He commanded a
day of rest from work (Exodus 31:15-17), giving principles of laboring for needs and thus condemning laziness. He gave laws for
dietary health and sanitation (Leviticus 11) by specifying foods

to avoid, bodily washing, and the disposal of waste. He gave commands for childbirth for the health of mother and child, He also established circumcision of the male child for the Israelites (Leviticus 12). He gave laws for disease and impurity (Leviticus 13-15) by separating the sick. Mankind benefits today from the principals given in God's word. The Bible continues to stand as the foundation to scientific knowledge.

Our Creator establishes His love for man in laws of morality given to protect us completely. Let me say in love and humility we must obey our God. Society pushes all to accept what clearly is condemned by our Maker. No matter how many attempts to portray immorality as normal, it is God, not man, who gave the Law. The soul looking to do right will obey what is already established. God warns of adultery and fornication throughout the Bible. Adultery breaks the sexual bond between husband and wife (Matthew 19:9). Fornication encompasses sexual sins including the unmarried (Colossians 3:5). God abhors homosexuality (Leviticus 20:13), of a man lying with a man as with a woman; women with women which is outside of nature (Romans 1:27). He prohibits incest (Deuteronomy 22:30, 27:22). He abhors bestiality (Exodus 22:19). He warns of drunkenness (Proverbs 20:1, 23:29-32). Also included in moral laws would be murder, the premeditated taking of an innocent human life (Genesis 9:6). This does not comprise an exhaustive list of scriptures but offers reference for the topics mentioned.

For every action there is a reaction. If one eats only candy and drinks only soda, the effects will be recognized in the body with obesity and diabetes. Our bodies react to the care or lack of care. The moral law given to man protects him in the laws of nature. Many sexual sins are exhibited in sexually transmitted diseases such as syphilis, HIV, and herpes. The sin of incest leads to physical traits in future generations such as misshaped skulls, protruding jaws, and dwarfism. As well, incest leads to a compromised immune system, infertility, or blood conditions such as hemophilia. Drunkenness or alcoholism becomes a disease effecting not only the one who drinks but those around that person. Heart, liver, and bone damage result from alcohol. Cognitive skills are hampered, eventually leading to damage in the brain. Coordination becomes compromised in balance and can damage muscle tissue. It is an addicting disease ruining lives by the constant need of the drink. In turn, the effects become apparent to others in anger and abuse (physical, verbal, and emotional).

At some point, the body will no longer function, whether by accident, disease, or age. Pneumonia takes the life of an infant. An automobile crash ends the life of a teenager. Congestive heart disease is the cause in the death of an elderly man. Science looks to discover means to prolong life by medicine or cryonics, yet all people eventually come to an end. The human body continues to astound those in the medical field with its intricacy and restorative ability. The Christian attributes all to God while the atheist tries to explain the design without the Designer.

Second, let us discuss the soul. It is the part of man and woman which contrasts the body in several points. The soul is our spiritual essence and not physical form. Our created condition can be thought of as a driver in a car. The car is the body and is controlled by the one inside. The driver inside is the soul. The driver sets the direction, speed, and destination under the limitations of the car. You control your action through your body under the limitations of your body. The car belongs to the driver but is not the driver. Your body belongs to you but it is not the individual you are inside – the soul.

Accurately, it is the part of each person which reveals her true self, emotions, thoughts, and determination. The command, written for us in Deuteronomy and Matthew, to love God with our soul involves the love coming from our inner self or being. God is love (1 John 4:8). The love that God has toward us is the highest form. That love wants the highest good for and from us. It brings quick correction and mercy. That love is universally offered even to enemies and betrayers. God wants what is best for our whole being and entire existence which is eternal. Love is from the soul. The soul is where it originates and is driven. Our love for God is expressed and verified by devotion and faith. It is shown by keeping His laws exactly as Christ described in John 14:15, **"If you love Me, keep My commandments."**

The soul cannot be seen. We can visually see the body and those bodies around us every day. However, the soul, being eternal and internal, is not observed with the eye. Unlike the body, the soul will not die and decompose. Solomon wisely says, **"Then the dust will return to the earth as it was, And the spirit will return to God who gave it"** (Ecclesiastes 12:7), recalling man's origin from the dust of the ground. The apostle Paul states, **"For this corruptible must put on incorruption, and this mortal must put on immortality"** (1Corinthians 15:53), describing how the earthly body transitions to the spiritual. It is the part to continue after the end of the body. Chapter fifteen logically contrasts the natural body to the spiritual body, teaching us flesh and blood cannot inherit the kingdom of God. Paul teaches a part of us will be changed to be in the heavenly realm. The body will remain on earth but the soul will go to Hades waiting for the Judgment Day. The destination of souls will be detailed and discussed further in a separate chapter.

Life on earth has challenges in our mortal body, but it is the vessel given us for our time on earth. How we use our body, whether to fulfill evil desire or glorify God through obedience, remains our task. Frailties in our physical health test our spiritual stamina in endurance. But by reading His word, it becomes a structure to lean upon, a foundation to build upon, and the precepts to guide our actions. Each soul has free will. Jesus encourages all in His sermon, **"Therefore I say to you, do not worry about your life, what you will eat or what you will drink; nor about your body, what you will put on. Is not life more than food and the body more than clothing?"** (Matthew 6:25). Jesus continues in the lesson to teach us of placing our priorities correctly: **"For your heavenly Father knows that you need all these things. But seek first the kingdom of God and His righteousness, and all these things shall be added to you"** (6:32-33). The soul will leave the physical body to exist into eternity. Seek the Lord first and obey what He says is right. Do you not want to be with your Lord forever?

> **"For our citizenship is in heaven, from which we also eagerly wait for the Savior, the Lord Jesus Christ, who will transform our lowly body that it may be conformed to His glorious body, according to the working by which He is able even to subdue all thing to Himself"** (Philippians 3:20-21).

CHAPTER FOUR: WHERE WILL THE SOUL GO?

C omfort rates a high priority. We purchase comfort shoes, comfort bedding, and comfort chairs to satisfy the ease we have come to expect and demand. If the room is too cold, the heat turns on. Should the room be too warm, air conditioning will adjust the temperature to a cool climate. When stepping out of a hot shower, our skin shivers until dry and warm with clothes. Viruses attack the body leaving us a reminder of how wonderful it is to be healthy. We take for granted how much of our day deals with adjustments to return to a comfortable feeling. Have you considered never knowing comfort again?

Recall the time you were the sickest, whether a flu, hospitalization, or treatment for a disease. You could never remember being so miserable and ill. Could things ever be so bad again? Then remember the occasion you were saddest; the loss of a child or spouse, a natural disaster which led to emotional ruin. How can you continue? Can you imagine a time the situation could be worse? Any emotion one can feel in this life- anger, fright, hatred, no matter the degree- will be nothing compared to how the lost soul will feel in eternity. From this existence, there is no relief.

What happens at death? At the point of one's death, the soul instantly goes to the realm referred to as *Hades*. This word appears only in the New Testament in the original Greek, while the Old Testament renders the same understanding as *Sheol* from the Hebrew. Hades (Sheol) is frequently confused with the everlasting punishment of Hell but is not the same. Hades comprises two places for souls until God's final judgment. Here the soul begins and understands its fate; it is like a waiting area. Every righteous soul appears in what is named *Paradise* (Luke 23:43) or *Abraham's bosom* (Luke 16:22). Jesus in forgiving one of the men beside Him at Golgotha stated, **"Assuredly, I say to you, today you will be with Me in Paradise"** (Luke 23:43), knowing they both were approaching death. Several scriptures name the places where souls will go.

> **"For you will not leave my soul in Sheol nor will You allow Your Holy One to see corruption"** (Psalm 16:10).

> **"I am He who lives, and was dead, and behold, I am alive forevermore. Amen. And I have the keys of Hades and of Death"** (Revelation 1:18).

> **"Then Death and Hades were cast into the lake of fire. This is the second death"** (Revelation 20:14).

Peter confesses Jesus as the Christ the Son of God. By this confession Jesus answers, **"And I also say to you that you are Peter, and on this rock I will build My church, and the gates of Hades shall not prevail against it"** (Matthew 16:18). Our Lord teaches us nothing will stop the church; not even death itself.

The other side of Hades where the unrighteous go is *torments*. **"And being in torments in Hades, he lifted up his eyes"** (Luke 16:23).

No scripture more clearly helps us understand where we go at the moment of death than Luke 16:19-31 where Jesus gives a historical account of two men. Jesus tells us of a certain rich man who lived his life luxuriously, while Lazarus, a beggar, lived a pitiable existence. The dogs of the city were alone in showing care for him by licking his sores. Though the rich man saw Lazarus, he never offered help to a fellow Jew. You can imagine how the rich man dressed well, ate sumptuously, and lived in a fine house. At the death of each man they are now in vastly different places; a real dwelling, not fabled ideas. Lazarus is carried by angels to what is named Abraham's bosom and comforted, while the rich man begins his eternal suffering in what is called torment. He began suffering thousands of years ago and continues to suffer to this day. Calling out to Abraham, the rich man begs for mercy, asking to send Lazarus with a drop of water for his tongue as he is in flames. Abraham points out the ironic turn of events as Lazarus is now comforted and the rich man is now miserable. Continuing, he also tells the rich man there is no way to reach across to him. In desperation, the man begs for Lazarus to go back to the living and warn his five brothers so they do not have the same end. Abraham reminds him the living have Moses and the prophets to hear, and even if one came back from the dead they would not be persuaded.

This passage has been misunderstood, being labeled as a parable instead of a true historical account. A closer study of the text shows it cannot be a parable for numerous reasons. Jesus is the perfect teacher, always giving the right answer and lesson to teach the disciples while on His earthly ministry. There would be no need to fabricate a story to make a point. He would be lying by quoting Abraham if the account were fictional. The reference of hearing Moses and the prophets would also be a lie. It would be misleading to teach us the righteous who die are carried by angels, if it were not reality. Jesus as part of the Godhead (God the Father, Jesus Christ the Son, and the Holy Spirit) cannot lie as taught in Titus (Titus 1:2).

Jesus teaches visually what happens after death. Those who obeyed God are carried by angels to a place of comfort where they will never again have contact with the earth. They will not be able to contact any living person. Still today charlatans swindle family and friends who look to reach out to a deceased loved one, hoping to hear all is well where they dwell. This is an impossibility. Tragically those who do not obey God lift their eyes in torments where they feel flames unendingly and the regret of their wasted life. We learn there is a great gulf between the two existences where no contact or exchange can be made. Souls tortured cannot come to the side of comfort. Life, now over, begins an eternal damnation at their last breath. Jesus also teaches the recognition of souls. The rich man knew Lazarus and called to Abraham who he would have never seen before. Though we are not given what form each soul appeared, the unrighteous rich man saw the righteous Lazarus and Abraham to his shame and misery.

What happens after death is a question asked by every generation. But the answer given continues to be ignored by most people for two reasons. First, the knowledge can be hurtful to think of loved ones who have already died in a terrifying existence with no way to rectify the situation. Buying a soul out of purgatory is a man-made denominational idea with no basis in the Biblical text. Second, once the truth in the scripture is understood, it requires action on their part and a change of life. People are comfortable in the life they live and find it difficult to make another commitment. Therefore, many choose the easy road to simply not believe the Bible. The choice, however, will not help their souls in the future or those who have already died in the past. Each soul has one opportunity to live his life until the Creator takes it back.

Heaven is the place all people, even those who do not claim God, want to go. On the day of judgment, the need of Hades will finish. It will be cast into the lake of fire. All souls from Adam to the last soul created, whether still living on the earth or waiting in Hades, will stand before Christ the Judge (2 Timothy 4:1-2, 8) and receive their reward of Heaven or Hell.

And the dead were judged according to their works, by the things which were written in the books. The sea gave up the dead who were in it, and Death and Hades delivered up the dead who were in them. And they were judged, each one according to his works. Then Death and Hades were cast into the lake of fire. This is the second death. And anyone not found written in the Book of Life was cast into the lake of fire (Revelation 20:12-15).

The hope which is laid up for you in heaven, of which you heard before in the word of the truth of the gospel (Colossians 1:5).

Blessed be the God and Father of our Lord Jesus Christ, who according to His abundant mercy has begotten us again to a living hope through the resurrection of Jesus Christ from the dead, to an inheritance incorruptible and undefiled and that does not fade away, reserved in heaven for you (1 Peter 1:3-4).

Heaven will be joy and light forevermore (Revelation 22:5). A living hope. An eternal home. Revelation 21:4 encourages, **"And God will wipe away every tear from their eyes; there shall be no more death, nor sorrow, nor crying. There shall be no more pain, for the former things have passed away."** The former things refer to their life on earth from which they are now free.

A cruise ship floundering in the Gulf of Mexico with power failure housed passengers texting to family of "hellish" conditions. Four days of overflowing toilets, spoiling food, and tropical heat would have been awful to endure. But to refer to this as "hellish" shows a lack of Biblical knowledge. Hell is a word used flippantly in our language today even by children who have not been taught to use proper speech. Most do not understand the eternal dwelling they are speeding toward. It is not just a curse word said in anger. Studying Bible scriptures reveals the very real, true, and sobering abode. How does the Bible describe hell?

Jesus describes hell like the enormous garbage dump outside Jerusalem - Gehenna. People of His day knew well of what He spoke with the continuing fire of burning trash. The souls of the wicked are described in a dreadful state of eternally rotting away in a place where there is always fire and torment. Hell is graphically visual for those who will take the Bible at its word. It is not a fabled land governed by a laughable, cartoonish character such as Santa from Christmas Town.

Several passages vividly show the real dwelling of lost souls. In Matthew 13:41-42, Jesus says, **"The Son of Man will send out His angels, and they will gather out of His kingdom all things that offend, and those who practice lawlessness, and will cast them into the furnace of fire. There will be wailing and gnashing of teeth."** This expresses the constant pain and unceasing torment one will endure. Jesus also warns us in Mark 9:45-46 of being **"cast into hell, into the fire that shall never be quenched- 'where Their worm does not die, And the fire is not quenched' "**. It is hard to imagine the unending decay but it is explained to us in an earthly concept for our realization of this punishment. Revelation 14:11 tells us **"the smoke of their torment ascends forever and ever; and they have not rest day or night, who worship the beast and his image, and whoever receives the mark of his name."** Never to have rest again is a foreign idea to us; however, the statement should shake us. Jesus tells us to truly respect and be afraid of God's judgment in Matthew 10:28: **"And do not fear those who kill the body but cannot kill the soul. But rather fear Him who is able to destroy both soul and body in hell."** The Hebrews writer warns us in Hebrews 10:30-31, **"For we know Him who said, 'Vengeance is Mine, I will repay,' says the Lord. And again, 'The LORD will judge His people.' It is a fearful thing to fall into the hands of the living God."** These passages in God's word are to be read with a sober mind and open heart.

Some souls do not live to thrive outside the mother's womb. I look forward to meeting a brother I never saw in this life as he died before birth. It was a crushing blow to my father who desperately wanted a son. My brother's soul is with God and is forever in Heaven. Some individuals celebrate a great milestone of living one hundred years or more. Souls are given various days or years- we have no say. Every twenty-four hours is a gift to use for good; we must not take blessings or opportunities for granted.

"Then the dust will return to the earth as it was, And the spirit will return to God who gave it" (Ecclesiastes 12:7).

Where will the soul go? King Solomon tells us in the book of Ecclesiastes it returns to God. He created and gave us the soul and He will judge where it will go by our obedience. The physical body returns to dust by decomposition, but the soul will never die. William M. Golden penned this encouraging hymn, *Where the Soul Never Dies*:

> *To Canaan's land I'm on my way, Where*
> *the soul of man never dies.*
> *My darkest night will turn to day, Where*
> *the soul of man never dies.*
> *No sad farewells, No tear-dimmed eyes*
> *Where all is love, And the soul of man never dies.*

CHAPTER FIVE: WHY DO
WE HAVE A SOUL?

Sipping the dark brew, she felt the secret pleasure. Cuban coffee from a demitasse cup was like drinking an exotic elixir from a dollhouse accessory. This inspired my lifetime love for the deliciously strong liquid. Daddy would let us have one sip. Just one for each of his three girls. It was enough to keep me wanting more. Ybor City is a Cuban section of Tampa. Going there was traveling to another world as a child. The heavy smell of garlic and hot Cuban bread, the sound of imported music, the sight of old brick buildings and sidewalks constructed in the late 1800's, the feel of the old wooden chairs, the taste of deviled crab with hot sauce ticked all senses. No other city in the U.S. can create authentic Cuban food. Picking up this unique cuisine proceeds seeing family. Yes, that good.

We are shaped by forces and influences throughout life and change in ways that may not be readily traceable. My parents both said they knew when I developed certain likes and dislikes. They witnessed it in action. But I am more than a collection of habits. Behaviors and habits change and quite often should change. There are plenty of things which enthralled me as a girl, but I outgrew them. Other interests may continue, but none of it defines me nor is it the person I am. Those things are all peripheral and are the evidence and result of the soul within. They are the decisions made by the person. Being a coffee drinker or appreciator of Cuban food does not identify who I am. I would still be me if the opposite were true – that I would avoid coffee and Cuban food. Actually, nothing would be different except a few tastes and yens. If my experiences and formative years were elsewhere, I would have a different set of likes and ways about me. There would still be me. I know my existence and my being proves something much greater than myself. The details of this have been written and protected for centuries. Therefore, the mystery of existence is no mystery at all.

A lovely composition has a composer, a beautiful painting has a painter, and an awe-inspiring creation has a Creator. Logic can be used in so many areas of life on earth but somehow tossed out and not applied to the spiritual. But the same logic applies to the Bible and its lessons in history, science, medical, law, morality, and religion. Approaching God's word with an open mind void of preconceived ideas proves the truth of the world around us.

Mankind asks "why?" continually. It is our nature. Books are written in the hope of imparting superior knowledge on various subjects, including books on how to ask questions. Why do we have a soul? Our Maker in His perfect wisdom designed man with a soul. Though man looks outward to find the reason, perhaps by worshipping the elements of earth or concocting myths of how people developed, yet the simple truth can be found in God's word. Consider three reasons: we are created in God's image, we are to glorify and worship Him, and our soul continues into eternal life.

Man is privileged to have a soul since God created him in His image. The sixth day of the creation week God formed man from the dust of the ground. He breathed into him the breath of life and he became a soul. With His love for man, God has given the Bible to mankind to instruct, encourage, and equip him because of his importance. Though the Creator filled the seas, sky, and land with creatures, only man has a soul. God created a vast array of animals, insects, and sea creatures, yet none of them are endowed with a soul. Those creations though intricate and splendid do not live on at death. They are unable to think, reason, and discern beyond their immediate need. Man alone was created in the image of God uniquely separate from the rest of creation.

"Yes, in the way of Your judgments, O Lord, we have waited for You; The desire of our soul is for Your name And for the remembrance of You. With my soul I

have desired You in the night, Yes, by my spirit within me I will seek You early; For when Your judgments are in the earth, The inhabitants of the world will learn righteousness" (Isaiah 26:8-9).

Man is privileged to have a soul to glorify and worship God. This is one of our main duties to our Creator. Scriptures verify this command throughout the Bible:**"that you may with one mind and one mouth glorify the God and Father of our Lord Jesus Christ"** (Romans 15:6). **"For you were bought at a price; therefore glorify God in your body and in your spirit, which are God's"** (1 Corinthians 6:20).

He has blessed us with all that is good and our gratitude should be conveyed. Foremost because He is our Creator, we should glorify and worship Him. Man needs and looks to worship. But he must worship correctly by the laws given for true worship by the Lawgiver. God, in giving the ten commandments to the Israelites recorded in Exodus 20, begins by telling them He is their God. They are to have no other god or to bow down and serve them. Specifically recorded for God's people, they are to not make carved images of any likeness of earthly things. He reminds them He brought them out of bondage in Egypt to give them a land of their own. The Egyptians carved and served many false gods over which our one true God demonstrated His power superior through ten plagues (Exodus 7:14 -12:30). Sadly, God's people turned away repeatedly with much of the Old Testament filled with the history of Israel rebelling and the punishment given for such sin. God tells us He is a jealous God in scripture and expects us to always put Him first.

"God is Spirit, and those who worship Him must worship in spirit and truth" (John 4:24).

Then Jesus said to him, "Away with you, Satan! For it is written, You shall worship the Lord your God, and Him only you shall serve" (Matthew 4:10).

Glorifying and worshipping God involve loving Him. Beside the command to love Him in Deuteronomy 6, as mentioned before, the book of John states the familiar scripture, **"For God so loved the world that He gave His only begotten Son, that whoever believes in Him should not perish but have everlasting life"** (John 3:16). In sacrificing His Son on the cross for mankind, no greater love has ever been shown. Through the many blessings abundantly given, we learn to love greater. The Bible teaches us He is our Father to encourage that love. My own father did not have a good father as an example and consequently was not affectionate to me and my sisters. He was a child of divorce torn apart from his parents as a young boy. But even with that hampered background, by his diligent care, we knew he greatly loved us. God in His word repeatedly tells us He loves us in word and deed.

In Psalm 42:1, there is a comparison made between the need for water and a thirst for God: **"As the deer pants for the water brooks, So pants my soul for You, O God."** Without water man will perish. Without God, man's spiritual state is doomed. This psalm, though written in beautiful poetic language, simply illustrates and compares physical needs to spiritual needs. It is a brilliant way of teaching. Another psalm speaks of the stability found in God: **"Unless the Lord had been my help, My soul would soon have settled in silence. If I say 'My foot slips,' Your mercy, O Lord will hold me up. In the multitude of my anxieties within me, Your comforts delight my soul"** (Psalm 94:17-19).

Peter teaches us **as newborn babes, desire the pure milk of the word, that you may grow thereby** (1 Peter 2:2), to crave God's word to help in our Christian walk just as a newborn needs milk. When I had my first child, I quickly discovered being a mother was not effortless and easy. I struggled with breastfeeding with our firstborn, nervously held him, and surely made mistakes. But I loved him so much the desire for his care outweighed any hesitation or fear. I learned to care for him because of my love for him. Desire evokes the intensity of our relationship with God. It is not to be a casual pastime one fits in our schedule as able, but instead an enveloping cloak we always keep on. God is worthy of our all.

In Matthew 22, Jesus repeats the command given by Moses. He verifies that the greatest commandment given to man is to love God with our all. These are direct commands and not suggestions to mankind to take or leave. Knowing the existent of His love and care for us brings the realization of love we should return. Again, that love was shown by giving His own Son as a sacrifice for each soul. The book of Hebrews in numerous verses teaches of Jesus' sacrifice for mankind as **"so Christ was offered once to bear the sins of many"** (Hebrews 9:28). Our supreme example, Jesus, suffered so much while on earth leaving lessons to give us strength to endure. Jesus knew His purpose given to Him by His Father as stated, **"Now My soul is troubled, and what shall I say? 'Father, save Me from this hour'? But for this purpose I came to this hour"** (John 12:27). No one will ever suffer as Jesus, whatever their trial in life.

> **"Looking unto Jesus, the author and finisher of our faith, who for the joy that was set before Him endured the cross, despising the shame, and has sat down at the right hand of the throne of God"** (Hebrews 12:2).

We glorify God through our obedience to His commands. God is a righteous lawgiver where what is asked is not a burden but for our benefit. In His wisdom He gives instruction and laws to help us navigate successfully our time on the earth. We glorify God by enduring suffering whether physical, emotional, or brought about by others' wickedness.

> **"Yet if anyone suffers as a Christian, let him not be ashamed, but let him glorify God in this matter"** (1 Peter 4:16).

"For this is the love of God, that we keep His commandments. And His commandments are not burdensome" (1 John 5:3).

Man is privileged to have a soul for it will continue in eternal life. Chapter Three spoke fully on the topic. Physical life on earth will only be the end of a body but the soul goes to the Hadean world awaiting judgment. Egyptian pharaohs had massive pyramids built to house furniture, statues, and weapons along with their wealth of gold and precious stone, believing they would need it in the afterlife. This material wealth remained in the tombs. Grave robbers stole the treasure which was of no use to the monarchs after their death. Truly you cannot take it with you. Given by the Master Teacher in Luke 12, Jesus uses a parable of a man unprepared for death prioritizing his material gain over his spiritual state.

"And I will say to my soul, 'Soul, you have many goods laid up for many years; take your ease; eat, drink, and be merry.' But God said to him, 'Fool! This night your soul will be required of you; then whose will those things be which you have provided?' " (Luke 12:19-20).

This rich man put all his effort in planning for many years, confident of having plenty and living well. No thought was given where he would be at his death. God wakes him up to reality in telling him time is over, his soul is required and his wealth does not come along. The state of being unprepared for death comes to the majority of mankind. Millions finish their lives in ignorance or disregard toward their Maker. Worldly wisdom focuses on man preparing a healthy retirement with his finances, planning for a house in a community of similar age neighbors, and enjoying recreational activities in his coming years. He believes he has many years to spend in easy living, reaping the benefit of his toil. Without God in his life plan, futility and ruin becomes the end. Souls need God. We need God. Our Creator calls us back to acknowledge Him, glorify and worship, love and obey, and prepare to meet Him in the last day. Above all else He is what we desire. This may be met with a scoff, but it is true nonetheless. We may not have come to realize it yet. Some may not want it to be true. But it is in our most basic purpose. When all else is stripped away, there remains our original design fully intact – our most basic need.

On a quiet afternoon in a very quiet house, I came across a photo. It caught my eye from a group of pictures. It was of an infant. She was probably four months old or younger lying flat on a blanket looking up at the camera. The blanket was white with a repeating pattern of something yellow. The baby had a haze of downy fuzz on a round head with small ears half hidden by pudgy cheeks. These met the tiny curve of a chin with no neck in sight. The arms were so perfectly chubby, smooth, and roundish they almost appeared like they were formed by a confectioner's craft, as though they were made of fondant or some rich icing which had been shaped by a baker and carefully placed. The shoulders were oblong and slightly raised with small fists held close. Her tummy was like a ball of bread dough set to rise. She was profoundly delicate, minute, soft and pure but skillfully and precisely fashioned by the gentlest of hands. It seems impossible for something this dainty to be flawlessly shaped down to the smallest details of nose and toes and fingernails all in miniature. It is mystifying and a wonder. How could something so utterly roly-poly be so sharply defined? This goes beyond beautiful. In this little, simple form is the combination of adorability, cuteness, and the luster of sublime innocence. In her there is no concept of harm. She is incapable of any action that is not tender and expecting attention to any need. She had a slight frown which gave her a bearing of seriousness, but from a baby this expression is immediately funny. Her head is turned slightly to the right, but her eyes are bright and directed straight at the camera.

It is the eyes. Everything in the photo is soft: the blanket, the light, the shadow, and the baby. Everything in the photo is soft except the gaze. The eyes were keen observers without perceivable brows. She watched with the focused intensity of keeping note of every detail. These are indeed the windows into the soul, and someone was home looking out onto the world. Infants are entirely observant. They desire to learn existence and they take it in. What does it hold? What does it hold for me? Everything is new including experience itself.

This infant, like all babies, is made of a substance not of this world but in the image of God. This is an unspoiled work of God. This someone is looking out with eyes watching intently. Here is someone showing the most fundamental needs and desires of humanity. The very critical anticipations of the human soul are exposed and may never be so easily seen again past these years of childhood and this side of eternity. At this tiny part of existence is a person at her most basic level: innocent, without baggage, without guile, without worry, but expecting what is the most important to us all. No infant can enunciate the needs, but all instinctively understand what is necessary for human existence, the very thing needed by the human soul. It is far more than food and shelter. It cannot be replaced by a toy. It is love. It is love and everything that encompasses. Where love is missing a baby feels utterly betrayed and abandoned in a world where good does not exist. But it is expected. This baby has total confidence she will be loved and cared for. All she can do is trust that those taking care of her will.

In these two eyes of a baby are the fundamental expectations and needs of all mankind – we are all the same and made of the same extraordinary substance. She wants love from those greater than her. While she expects it from everyone, that is not as essential as the love from her parents. She wants acceptance that she is someone, and that she matters. She wants to be part of a loving family with the peace and stability it brings. Though she cannot possibly explain it, she knows when love is shown in the simplest form of compassion and she knows when it is missing.

For all who have grown beyond the childhood years, we can become controlled by ambition, craftiness, selfishness, pride, vindictiveness, and ruled by desires. Heaven brings us to what our souls actually want: love from the One greater than us, our Creator. We want to be part of a loving family. We want to be accepted as someone and to know that we matter. Everyone wants a home. In heaven every yearning of the soul is fulfilled to overflowing. In Heaven the soul finds home. The soul is welcomed into the place where God has always wanted us to be. Here is contentment, accomplishment, and deep satisfaction. The core and essential desires and purpose of the soul is supplied so richly it is beyond abundance.

Hell is a different conclusion. Hell is to be cast away and forever abandoned as nameless, worthless, and utterly forgotten in an endless existence separated from the One we want the most. The expression of a baby reveals what we really need and desire. In that gaze is the wide-eyed path into the soul. It reveals what we are: a soul wanting nothing more than love and approval from the Creator. A baby cannot explain it but knows instinctively when needs are met or denied. We all know when someone holds us as a treasure, or we have been cast away. It matters. When all the baggage and deception and clutter of this world have been removed, then we will see all that ever mattered was the love of God.

Then Jesus called a little child to Him, set him in the midst of them, and said, "Assuredly, I say to you,

unless you are converted and become as little children, you will by no means enter the kingdom of heaven. Therefore whoever humbles himself as this little child is the greatest in the kingdom of heaven. Whoever receives one little child like this in My name receives Me" (Matthew 18:2-5).

CHAPTER SIX: THE ESSENTIAL
BOOK IN THE LIBRARY

A math book is used to learn mathematics. One plus one equals two and no one denies the fact. A science book teaches about atoms to galaxies to living things. To master the role of Hamlet an actor must first read the play. The words spoken by the character must be memorized exactly to give justice to Shakespeare's work. Any college course taken comes with written words to learn and knowledge to retain. Books are seen as useful and are necessary to learn what is needed. But what book is there for moral living? In what text can we understand our purpose in existing? What book is there that can solve every possible human problem? There is a book and it is not from a textbook company. It is from God. What greater expert could there be on everything? His book would have to be the best possible book with all the correct answers. It has been given and preserved through the ages for us to know the most important things for our lives. Here is something so reliable you can build your life from the very words. It is, of course, the Bible. While everything else has come and failed, the Bible remains as it always has. There are no new editions. There are no corrections from discovered information. There are no new ideas. It needs no help. Its words are effective, and people know it. Why then do most show indifference to the Bible? It is typically seen as unnecessary with its teaching and facts unimportant. People live as though the enemies of the Bible never fail and it had never been proven perfect in every generation!

I learned to read at age four to keep up with my older sister. She would bring home books from first grade and I could not get enough of any story in her bookbag. Thrilled with the new ideas, alphabet, and pictures, reading came easy so I looked forward to my turn to attend first grade. Later in the sixth grade I endured a long bus ride to school and back again using the time to read. Sadly, it is not a love I continued. Dutifully reading the required school textbooks, somewhere my joy of reading evaporated. Still, I know reading is vital. Actually, our home has six tall bookcases. Full of cookbooks, novels, and children's literature they also contain many copies of the God-given book. Other homes probably have this world's best-selling book on their shelf which may be an heirloom copy or an inexpensive paperback version. Perhaps crowded and lost among popular fiction series, self-help books, and dictionaries, often no one has read it. Yet it is the essential book in any library whether on a family bookshelf or the Library of Congress – the Bible.

The Bible can be proven in facts of history, science, astronomy, geography, medicine, and more. But too many see it as an archaic book with no relevance. Few align its significance to philosophical reading, believing other men's work superior. Many apply their own thoughts and feelings when reading the Bible and disregard the truth of the text. Can that be said of an algebra book? Does anyone read *Huckleberry Finn* and believe personal thoughts will change the outcome of the original story? However, the Bible, which is the word of God, is subjected to millions believing their conscience outweighs His words which contains a given law for mankind. How arrogant for man to think himself above his Creator! This attitude has a name in the book of Proverbs: **"He who trusts in his own heart is a fool"** (Proverbs 28:26).

Satan instigates the sinful ideas of man to ignore what the Bible teaches. His temptation to delete God from each individual's mind causes the wickedness seen in the world. Most want to live in peace. Most want a world without crime. They want to be around decent people and to be good people. Most do not want to be a slave to sin, but they do not want the real solution. The answer can only be reached by following God's way. That is found in the one place most do not want to go – the Bible. God offers but man disregards. Thus man creates his own way of dealing with the problems of sin but he is utterly helpless. The problems remain and escalate. God gave the solution in a divine yet simple book but man does not want it.

For since the creation of the world His invisible *attributes* are clearly seen, being understood by the things that are made, *even* His eternal power and Godhead, so that they are without excuse, because, although they knew God, they did not glorify *Him* as God, nor were thankful, but became futile in their thoughts, and their foolish hearts were darkened. Professing to be wise, they became fools (Romans 1:20-22).

Solomon taught in Ecclesiastes 12:12, **"Of making books there is no end, and much study is wearisome to the flesh."** He refers to the vast knowledge men may attain which can become vanity without a higher goal. Truly he spoke right of the infinite number of books continually created. However, even the number one book on a coveted list eventually ends in the bargain bin no matter how many copies sold. With extensive choices and enormous competition, books published must have instant allure in a short-attention-span society. What appeal does a book written approximately 2000 years ago have for man today?

First, it answers the age-old question "Why am I here?" The question is primary and needs the correct answer. You cannot ignore your own existence. The fact you exist is immediately proven outright. The act of seeking proof of existence is proof enough. You exist – the nonexistent never ask questions. To ask "why?" is a soul wondering at his own purpose in being. Why am

I here rather than not here? Here I am cognizant, sentient, self-aware, and independent of the rest of creation. Now what? One has to admit a lot of energy has been put forth to bring this material realm into being and kept in perfect order: earth, sea, sky, plants, planets, animals, humanity. Did it need to include me? This question is an obvious one and universal to mankind because we share the same condition. The truth is: on your own you cannot really know. You can certainly make up a purpose for your existence such as, "I'm just here for the food." While that may be enjoyable, is it really why you were created? The earth and universe were created so you could enjoy the food. It seems a bit shallow and self-serving. Viktor Frankl's book *Man's Search for Meaning* acknowledges we must be here for a reason and must seek out that purpose. There must be something much larger than me and that is why I am here. Solomon wrote the book of Ecclesiastes in the same search at about 900 BC. This is a very ancient question. Is it mirth, feasts, and parties? Is it collecting and building amazing things? He searches to find what **"was good for the sons of men to do under heaven all the days of their lives"** (Ecclesiastes 2:3). He comes to the conclusion at the end of the book. It is the conclusion that we could not know without help. Why am I here? That question begs for a purpose because a purpose is hardwired into our souls. He gives the answer. **Let us hear the conclusion of the whole matter. Fear God and keep His commandments, For this is man's all** (Ecclesiastes 12:13). That is a healthy purpose. It is to serve the One who created us.

For ages man has tried to find ways of explaining his existence with fables and imaginative stories. Unashamedly, the beginning of the Bible states God is. It then logically and chronologically tells us He creates everything good in six days. In simple precise language, God lays the fact before the reader to help understand our world. Beginning from what was made each day, man's creation, the history of nations and, most important, how our Savior, Jesus Christ, is key to all. Earth and universe are created for man to use and benefit from. Man is the center of all creation and his redemption back to God is the plot of the book. In reading the Bible we learn God is worthy of our love and devotion. He formed us out of love in His image to serve and glorify Him.

Second, it speaks the truth. How many books written are brimming with hatred and lies which the unassuming reader believe as truth? Autobiographies of corrupt dictators, political men with vendettas, and history recorded incorrectly by those ignorant or with selfish ends all pen books full of inaccuracies. But the Bible is truth throughout all sixty-six books collected in one work. Historically it has been proven correct in geography, history, science, medical knowledge, and military warfare. Though ridiculed in the past for perceived discrepancies, the truth comes forward to show the validity of this unique book. Jesus states in John 8:32, **"And you shall know the truth, and the truth shall make you free."** This truth comes only from reading the Bible and following the commands given by God.

In this accurate text of history, men, women, and nations are displayed in all their sordid dealings and treacherous lives. It is not a fictional tale written of one man's story, but thousands of real historic people dealing with the remarkable situations in which they find themselves. What will happen to the eight family members with a cargo ship of animals staying afloat in a crashing flood? How does Joseph get out of a pit his own brothers threw him in to die? Does David escape the crazed king of Israel? What happens to the one who betrays Jesus? The answer comes to each of the questions, but you need to read the book. Yet, so many more accounts fill the pages to satisfy a lifetime of reading. Those unfamiliar with the Bible wrongly believe it a story of perfect mortals manipulated by a controlling elderly God. If this book were read with an open mind, the reader would learn of a loving Father who remains longsuffering to all. You would understand a perfect plan from the beginning to bring mankind back to his

God, how a chosen nation endured to keep a blood line pure to bring the Savior into the world. Christians who suffered beatings because of their faith are told as examples to believers today. This is but a fraction of what makes the Bible so vital for every soul to read.

Third, it teaches moral living. The Bible brings to light the commands of God for our good in all moral parts of our lives. It teaches in Genesis how singular in God's mind He formed man, giving him purpose. Made in His image, we have dominance over creatures and the earth. God had a plan from the beginning for man's salvation and a home in heaven. God gives us guidance in His laws for our safety in what we eat, how to deal with others individually, and how to govern a people. Again in Genesis, He establishes the institution of home and family with husband and wife then children if blessed. The union of man and woman in marriage keeps one from sexual sin and forms a lifelong bond of love and friendship. Children born into a family have stability and direction from their parents when taught in the Lord. Though the Bible has examples of families with frailties and imperfections, God still gave the laws to obey. It takes reading God's word to learn the principles. It is critical information.

In Leviticus the scriptures warn against false idol worship in the sinful practices associated with child sacrifice and fornication. Scriptures show, as God's people turn from His law to imitate worldly nations, they fall into horrific practices. Parents burned their children alive on the image of a false god as an act of worship. Men and women used sexual acts to worship idols as though it were a holy offering. Repeatedly God commands His people not to commit such practices.

As time marches on, man moves further away from the original plan laid out by God his Creator. Many more people today do not attend any worship service or know any Bible scriptures, choosing instead to remain entertained than instructed. It has led to more crime, abuse, divorce, and ignorance in our world. When a child does not receive instruction of basic Bible facts in how loved they are, the purpose in life, good and evil, and what awaits after death, they grow away from a good nature to learn worldly vices. Without the knowledge of moral living given by God, man reaps evil consequences to his demise.

My parents died in the same year, the same summer. They left behind a two-story house lived in for forty-eight years from an enduring marriage of fifty-eight years. On an acre wooded lot, it held memories of making furniture with the driveway pine straw, bouncing on a Space Hopper around the yard, and upgrading to a bigger bedroom as an older sister left the nest. We possessed the most beautiful manicured lawn which we girls helped with on Saturdays by raking, weeding, and mowing. At the time, the weekly chore seemed unfair, but with maturity I see it was valuable training in developing work ethic and family duty. Saturday evening was a banquet of grilled steak and handmade fries for the effort. I thrived in a privileged childhood. Eventually, this cherished home was floor to ceiling full of stuff. It became a daunting task to pick up each item, consider its worth, and categorize it as keeping or donating. Mother kept everything and continued to acquire until the end. By everything, this included stacks of plastic butter containers to a pantry of paper towels from the early 1970s. I considered contacting the Smithsonian to ask if it was eligible for a collection. She would be labeled a hoarder, but I know the condition came from living through the Great Depression and the dread of saying goodbye. That dread shifted from people to material things. However, in her holding on to items, I retrieved my first grade Walt Disney World lunchbox, a valuable Battling Tops game, and delicate homemade dresses my daughter was able to wear. Daddy was a high school and college football player, served in the military, and was an architect as profession. After retirement, he grew greenhouses full of the exotic plant Bromeliad, traveled extensively out west, and took up coin collecting. Mother was a homemaker: an excellent cook, expert seamstress, and a master gardener. Needless to say, the house moaned with the weight of books from all the combined interests. Ultimately, loved or not, possessions find other owners.

Bookcases full of books which garner some knowledge and momentary diversion basically are dust collectors. Do not let God's word, the Bible, be among those. It is the essential book in the library and must be daily studied.

CHAPTER SEVEN: THE GIFT
OF SALVATION

All people love to receive gifts. As children, an approaching birthday or Christmas brings expectation for toys begged and pleaded for. In the mind of a child, these must be given because it is expected. I remember my parents' gift of my first bicycle. Being the youngest I tended to receive hand-me-downs. Opening the trunk of the family car revealed a shiny new bike with a banana seat and streamers on the handlebars which was all the rage. Later as young parents, William and I ventured into Black Friday sales to purchase gifts for our three children at amazing prices, hoping to return uninjured. Waking up at four in the morning to save five dollars on a toy is absurd. What were we thinking? Sometimes what seemed vastly important then is now remembered vaguely or best forgotten. I anticipated the joy on my children's faces as they opened gifts. Material gifts can be precious, but how much more a gift from our Creator? All people have been given a tremendous gift, but few open the contents to examine it with any interest. It is a gift so wonderful, words come short of its worth.

What if you spent years producing a gift which took precious resources and agonizing effort? The person receiving this would obviously be one you love greatly. What if this gift was the very thing necessary to help that person for the rest of his life and was irreplaceable? What if this took everything you had to create, including your own life in the process? But what if the gift was despised? What if the person who received it saw it as nothing? What if they walked away from it as though it were unworthy of a moment's attention? The only answer to this is to fathom the level of contempt of this person, the ignorance and utter waste of effort for someone so foolish and thoughtless. But untold numbers of people have done this with the invaluable gift from their Creator. God has given all people the gift of salvation, but few look inside and most hatefully reject it.

To learn of salvation, we need to read the essential book which teaches thoroughly. This chapter will have many scripture references to completely prove each point. God's word teaches perfectly where any thoughts I may have are less important. Historically, man has interjected his own doctrines into the Bible which scripture does not teach (Galatians 1:8). The steps of salvation can be easily understood and followed from scripture only. The scriptures on subjects like salvation are quite clear. Scripture will answer every question of who, what, when, where, and how. It does so in a mastery of words.

Why do you need salvation? Because we all sin. Sin means to miss the mark, or we have violated a command of God. Man sinned from the beginning when Eve disobeyed God's command and Adam joined her (Genesis 3:6). Mankind, throughout the ages, continues to sin. **"For all have sinned and fall short of the glory of God"** (Romans 3:23), and **"For the wages of sin is death, but the gift of God is eternal life in Christ Jesus our Lord"** (Romans 6:23). A soul cannot return to God in sin, thus the need for salvation.

First, you must hear the message of God's word. You must learn what to do to obey the command. Jesus states in John 5:24, **"Most assuredly, I say to you, he who hears My word and believes in Him who sent Me has everlasting life, and shall not come into judgment, but has passed from death into life."** Jesus also gave the appeal, **"He who has ears to hear, let him hear"** (Matthew 11:15). He offers this plea multiple times. Why? Something important was just said and we need to pay attention. It had been the problem of the majority in Israel. Historically, most would not listen to the prophets before Jesus, including John the Baptist. Jesus addresses the churches of Asia in the book of Revelation with the command to listen in chapters two and three. Certainly, we have ears. He does not make a ridiculous statement. Our Lord tells us we must listen to His words. He is describing the fact that people can have two perfectly good ears and yet not listen. They may give everything else in life their attention and ignore what is needed the most, the message of salvation. Jesus then quotes a prophecy in Isaiah which stated there would be plenty refusing to be taught. They would block Jesus' words from their minds. In Matthew 13:14-15 Jesus quotes Isaiah 6:9-10. He applies the prophecy to those He has been trying to teach.

And in them the prophecy of Isaiah is fulfilled, which says:
"Hearing you will hear and shall not understand,
And seeing you will see and not perceive;
For the hearts of this people have grown dull.
Their ears are hard of hearing,
And their eyes they have closed,
Lest they should see with their eyes and hear with their ears,
Lest they should understand with their hearts and turn,
So that I should heal them."

The question then is this: do we listen or have our hearts grown dull?

The apostle Paul in a letter to the young preacher Timothy notes that learning God's word should begin early in life. **"And that from childhood you have known the Holy Scriptures, which are able to make you wise for salvation through faith which is in Christ Jesus"** (2 Timothy 3:15).

Paul also tells Timothy that the Lord gave him strength so he could continue preaching **and that all the Gentiles might hear** (2 Timothy 4:17). The greater portion of the world's population is Gentile. The idea **"that all the Gentiles might hear"** means the gospel was opened to the entire world. It was never meant for one people but is for **all nations, tribes, peoples, and tongues** (Revelation 7:9).

How then shall they call on Him in whom they have not believed? And how shall they believe in Him of

whom they have not heard? And how shall they hear without a preacher? (Romans 10:14).

Hearing and believing go hand in hand. Once the teaching is heard, it is upon the hearer to believe and develop faith. This is not a miraculous event. It is simple and a matter of personal conviction. We are to believe God is our Creator and His Son, Jesus, died for our sins. The Bible (from Genesis to Revelation) has one author. It is God. He worked through various prophets in different times to complete the Bible with its sixty-six books in about 1,400 years. Each book in the Bible was brought forth in the time needed with a purpose and initial audience. The Bible stands complete and has been protected and kept through the centuries for the saving of souls. The first four books of the New Testament, or gospel accounts, tell of the life of Jesus while on the earth. Matthew is a book written to the Jews as its initial audience. Mark focuses on Jesus the servant. Luke wrote to the Greeks. John wrote to both Jews and Greeks, focusing on Jesus as Deity. These four books together teach the scope of Jesus' life from before His birth to after His death on the cross. We are not called to an unfounded belief. We are called with sound words and evidence pointing to a logical conclusion. These are written to convince the hearer of the truth. Jesus cannot more plainly state the necessity of believing than recorded in the book of Mark, **"He who believes and is baptized will be saved; but he who does not believe will be condemned"** (Mark 16:16).

He who believes in the Son has everlasting life; and he who does not believe the Son shall not see life, but the wrath of God abides on him (John 3:36).

For I am not ashamed of the gospel of Christ, for it is the power of God to salvation for everyone who believes, for the Jew first and also for the Greek (Romans 1:16).

The writer of the Hebrews letter warns, **"But without faith**

it is impossible to please Him, for he who comes to God must believe that He is, and that He is a rewarder of those who diligently seek Him" (Hebrews 11:6). However, belief alone without obedience cannot save. James teaches in his book, **"You believe that there is one God. You do well. Even the demons believe -- and tremble!"** (James 2:19).

Once we believe in God and His Son, we are to realize our sinfulness and repent of the life we have led. On the day of Pentecost, fifty days after Jesus was on the cross, Peter and the other eleven apostles preached how to be saved. The same words of repentance apply to us today.

> **Then Peter said to them, "Repent, and let every one of you be baptized in the name of Jesus Christ for the remission of sins; and you shall receive the gift of the Holy Spirit"** (Acts 2:38).

> **For godly sorrow produces repentance leading to salvation, not to be regretted; but the sorrow of the world produces death** (2 Corinthians 7:10).

> **"I tell you, no; but unless you repent you will all likewise perish"** (Luke 13:5).

> **"Truly, these times of ignorance God overlooked, but now commands all men everywhere to repent, because He has appointed a day on which He will judge the world in righteousness by the Man whom He has ordained. He has given assurance of this to all by raising Him from the dead"** (Acts 17:30-31).

Confessing Jesus as our Lord and Savior is the next important step for a soul to be saved. We must have that as a personal conviction and be willing to state our belief. This is expected in obeying God. More than saying the words, it must be part of our being, loving Christ as He loves us. In a wedding ceremony the bride and groom willingly and openly confess their love for each other. It would be strange if they were unwilling to make that admission. Something would be amiss. In a courtroom, a willing witness will confess what they know pertinent to the case. Genuine devotion does not hesitate in speaking out what you know to be true and what you love. Christians in the first century willingly faced death for confessing Christ as God and not Caesar. Jesus tells us plainly how critical confessing is in our faith.

> **"Therefore whoever confesses Me before men, him I will also confess before My Father who is in heaven. But whoever denies Me before men, him I will also deny before My father who is in heaven"** (Matthew 10:32-33).

> **That if you confess with your mouth the Lord Jesus and believe in your heart that God has raised Him from the dead, you will be saved. For with the heart one believes unto righteousness, and with the mouth confession is made unto salvation** (Romans 10:9-10).

The act of baptism has been misunderstood in so many respects since commanded by Christ: its importance, practice, and necessity. Returning to the Koine Greek, the original language of the New Testament, the word *baptize* or *baptism* was transliterated into English from the Greek word βαπτίζω (baptizo). That Greek word means immersion or dip. Baptism is compared to a death in Colossians 2:12: **"buried with Him in baptism, in which you also were raised with Him through faith in the working of God, who raised Him from the dead."** The book of Acts recounts the early church, beginning with the day of Pentecost in chapter two. Through the chapters, it details specific examples of people being saved and baptism being involved in their salvation. No one verse gives all the steps of salvation, but taken as a whole, the commands are understood. It was not from any miraculous deed but by obeying the word of God that people were saved. **"And with many other words he testified and exhorted them, saying, 'Be saved from this perverse generation.' Then those who gladly** received his word were baptized; and that day about three thou-sand souls were added to them" (Acts 2:40-41).

> But when they believed Philip as he preached the things concerning the kingdom of God and the name of Jesus Christ, both men and women were baptized. Then Simon himself also believed; and when he was baptized he continued with Philip, and was amazed, seeing the miracles and signs which were done (Acts 8:12-13).

> And he brought them out and said, "Sirs, what must I do to be saved?" So they said, "Believe on the Lord Jesus Christ, and you will be saved, you and your household." Then they spoke the word of the Lord to him and to all who were in his house. And he took them the same hour of the night and washed their stripes. And immediately he and all his family were baptized (Acts 16:30-33).

> Then Crispus, the ruler of the synagogue, believed on the Lord with all his household. And many of the Cor-inthians, hearing, believed and were baptized (Acts 18:8).

Peter makes a direct comparison between baptism and the ark built by Noah as the means of salvation and obedience. If Noah was to survive the flood, he had to obey God in all things. So too, we must obey God in all things to be saved. The ark and baptism are compared as the means of salvation in two distinct times: the ark for the flood and baptism for today. "**Who formerly were disobedient, when once the Divine longsuffering waited in the days of Noah, while the ark was being prepared, in which a few, that is, eight souls, were saved through water. There is also an antitype which now saves us -- baptism (not the removal of the filth of the flesh, but the answer of a good conscience toward God), through the resurrection of Jesus Christ**" (1 Peter 3:20-21).

Many scriptures teach that faith is to be matched with good works. Good works are expected. They are demanded. Why would God call us to be exactly what we have always been? If that were the case, then there would be no call needed. God calls us to become the people He designed us to be.

> **For by grace you have been saved through faith, and that not of yourselves; *it is* the gift of God, not of works, lest anyone should boast. For we are His workmanship, created in Christ Jesus for good works, which God prepared beforehand that we should walk in them** (Ephesians 2:8-10).

> **You see then that a man is justified by works, and not by faith only** (James 2:24).

> **For the grace of God that brings salvation has appeared to all men, teaching us that, denying ungodliness and worldly lusts, we should live soberly, righteously, and godly in the present age** (Titus 2:11-12).

"For whoever calls on the name of the Lord shall be saved" (Romans 10:13). This is a verse that many denominational teachers use but are mistaken in what is meant by **"calls on the name of the Lord."** Paul quoted what God said through Joel: **"And it shall come to pass that whoever calls on the name of the Lord shall be saved. For in Mount Zion and in Jerusalem there shall be deliverance, As the Lord has said, Among the remnant whom the Lord calls"** (Joel 2:32). He was teaching there was no distinction between Jew and Greek to be saved. All were now offered salvation. Peter, at the beginning of the church, taught those at Pentecost the words of Joel were being fulfilled that day (Acts 2:16-21). Joel prophesied about the last days, the Christian age in which we live. To "call on the name of the Lord" encompasses obedience to all the steps commanded for salvation. Belief and baptism are linked together as in the conversion of Saul who later becomes the apostle Paul. Ananias instructs him to obey the command of God, **"And now why are you waiting? Arise and be baptized, and wash away your sins, calling on the name of the Lord"** (Acts 22:16). Ananias tells Saul that he was still in his sins. Saul already met Christ on the road to Damascus. Christ told Ananias the purpose He had for Saul. Yet Saul was still in sin. The problem of his sins had to be solved. At this point in his life, did Saul have no faith that Jesus was Lord? He had to. Christ told Saul who He was in Acts 9:5: **"And he said, 'Who are You, Lord?' Then the Lord said, 'I am Jesus, whom you are persecuting. It is hard for you to kick against the goads.'"** There could be no doubt that Saul would have believed Jesus. Jesus is Lord. But when Saul makes his way into Damascus he is still in his sins. He had yet to obey all that is required from all of us. In Acts 22:16 baptism is associated with washing away sins and calling on the name of the Lord. When Saul is baptized, he completes the steps to salvation. He is saved by obedience, or in other words, he called on the name of the Lord.

> **Therefore, my beloved, as you have always obeyed, not as in my presence only, but now much more in my absence, work out your own salvation with fear and trembling** (Philippians 2:12).

Once baptism has taken place, your life as a Christian must still be active. Being immersed in water is not the end. We are not to return to our previous lives of sin. We must diligently work on staying saved by living righteously. The writer of the book of Hebrews warns us that a heavenly home can be lost: **"Therefore, since a promise remains of entering His rest, let us fear lest any of you seem to have come short of it"** (Hebrews 4:1). We are called to be faithful unto death (Revelation 2:10) and overcome. Christians must share their faith and win souls for Jesus so others can have a home in heaven. Salvation comes through Jesus Christ as taught repeatedly in scripture.

> **Nor is there salvation in any other, for there is no other name under heaven given among men by which we must be saved** (Acts 4:12).

For if when we were enemies we were reconciled to God through the death of His Son, much more, having been reconciled, we shall be saved by His life (Romans 5:10).

For God did not appoint us to wrath, but to obtain salvation through our Lord Jesus Christ (1 Thessalonians 5:9).

And having been perfected, He became the author of eternal salvation to all who obey Him (Hebrews 5:9).

From an early age, songs help in learning or memorizing information, whether the alphabet, multiplication tables, or state capitals. The rhythm of the tune connects with the words to be remembered making an easy task. This tool works well in memorizing Bible verses. Spiritual songs or hymns are used in worship to God to teach and admonish (Colossians 3:16). They can center the mind on difficult subjects. Carrie Breck (1855-1934), a homemaker and mother of five children, wrote some of the most beautiful hymns still sung today. We can read Bible passages often, yet not consider the magnitude of the subject. But with few words penned to the hymn, she perfectly conveys our personal debt and the selfless love of our Savior in giving His life. I have always been unable to sing these words without crying.

Nailed to the Cross

There was One who was willing to die in my stead,
That a soul so unworthy might live;
And the path to the cross He was willing to tread,
All the sins of my life to forgive.
He is tender and loving and patient with me, While
He cleanses my heart of its dross,
But "there's no condemnation"- I know I am free,
For my sins are all nailed to the cross.
I will cling to my Savior and never depart, I will joyfully

journey each day,
With a song on my lips and a song in my heart,
That my sins have been taken away.
They are nailed to the cross! They are nailed to the
cross! O how much He was willing to bear!
With what anguish and loss, Jesus went to the cross!
But He carried my sins with Him there.

CHAPTER EIGHT: WINNING SOULS

"It is in the details. Pay attention to what you have done and what is needed."

T ypically, when I asked one of my children to clean a room, they would obey, but probably not to my liking. Admittedly, I can be slightly compulsive about a spotless home, but I see this as normal. They usually tidied it in a hurried manner then reported to me when the job was accomplished. They believed the area clean. They felt confident they had done the job. A parent's internal quality control sees differently. To the child it is as though there is mischievous magic about the house. The pile of clothes in the corner, the things left on the floor, or dirty dishes on the kitchen counter only appear when a parent enters the room. The words, "How did that get there?" are spoken with complete astonishment and have been heard in our house over the years. The truth is: the room they thought was clean was not clean. The job was not done; as a matter of fact, it had hardly begun. There is a difference between a clean room and a dirty room we think clean. The difference will be found in the details. "Those things on the floor you walk around or trip over must be picked up." That is a detail. These various particulars matter – even the ones we consider small. Why am I using this illustration? Is that not what God tells us throughout scripture? We must pay attention to what we are doing and how we are doing it. This is a call and expectation for full commitment. Obedience to God is not to be done casually or superficially. We have a moral responsibility of true discipleship. He is worthy of all of our attention. God is either worth all our heart, soul, mind, and strength (Mark 12:30) or He is worth nothing. There are plenty of times Jesus teaches an expected level of faithfulness. In Matthew 12:30, He says, **"He who is not with Me is against Me, and he who does not gather with Me scatters abroad."** Saul of Tarsus believed himself to be committed to full obedience to God. His conscience was clear and his intentions sincere (Acts 23:1). He thought he served God, but the reality and outcome of his work was at the other end of the scale. Instead of obeying God, Saul was persecuting God (Acts 9:5). Instead of gathering, Saul was ignorantly scattering. To scatter with a clear conscience is still scattering and working against Christ. Good intentions cannot change this. With God's grace Saul receives the truth, obeys in baptism, and becomes an apostle, Paul, bearing the name of Christ **"before Gentiles, kings, and the children of Israel"** (Acts 9:15). God sends us to the job and He gives the specifics for the work. We understand that in life. The automobile assembled on the line at the Nissan plant must have all its parts for the car to properly function. Film and television productions employ a continuity supervisor to ensure details are seamless from one shot to the next. Why not use logic and attention to detail in His commands as well?

Details matter to God. Paying attention to detail in God's word means the difference of obeying or disobeying. It means the difference between life and death. Eve learned that the detail in God's command mattered (Genesis 3). Nadab and Abihu learned that the detail in worship to God mattered (Leviticus 10). Uzzah and David learned that the detail in the laws for moving the Ark of the Covenant mattered (2 Samuel 6). Death was the result in all of this. Adam and Eve died spiritually the moment they sinned. Nadab and Abihu died on the spot for their neglect of one detail. Uzzah was killed by the wrath of God because he touched the Ark of the Covenant. Even though Uzzah had the best of intentions, he did what God forbade. God gave warning concerning the Ark in the days of Moses in Numbers 4:15. God means what He says. Mankind wants to think of God as an easygoing grandfather who will give in for any mistakes made. He will accept any behavior we choose. Even those who have read the scriptures focus on the verses of love and grace, believing His love will cover a multitude of sins. God is love; of that truth there is no doubt. He is also absolute justice and gave perfect laws. Our system of law finds loopholes, plea bargains, reduced sentences, and corrupt judges which diminish faith in receiving fair trials. The number of laws in the United States cannot be numbered just in state and federal laws which change by year. However, God's word does not change. It will not alter based on current trends, popular thought or political leaning. You can have faith and base your life on the Bible.

When we see a current movie, hear a popular song, or eat in a fantastic local restaurant we want to share the news with family and friends. It should be even more so with sharing the Gospel which means *good news*. Introducing the Bible to another could lead to the saving of her soul and perhaps other souls. It is worth speaking up. Understand, many people are completely unfamiliar with the content of the scriptures, hearing only what others wrongly believe or misunderstand. The courage in approaching one about his faith could change a life. Not all will be agreeable to discussing biblical topics, but the effort must be taken. Every soul is precious to God. The number of souls from the creation of Adam to now is innumerable, yet God knows each one and cares as a parent for his child. A caring mother nourishes a love for her children while they are yet unborn and continues to see to their needs as they grow. God, being our Father and Creator, has a far greater love for each soul. In the New Testament John teaches, **"We love Him because He first loved us"** (1 John 4:19). Since it has been established how vital the soul is and what awaits each of us in eternity, the Christian must take every opportunity to teach and warn others. When you have important life changing information you must share it. Part of glorifying God with our lives is to win souls. This is a primary duty.

The fruit of the righteous is a tree of life, And he who wins souls is wise (Proverbs 11:30).

We should be active in winning souls because of the value of each. Our family visited Washington D.C., seeing all the many museums and monuments. In the National Museum of Natural

History, we peeked at the Hope Diamond through the crowds. At over forty-five carats, the largest blue diamond has an estimated worth of two hundred fifty million dollars. It has exchanged ownership many times with no individual possessing it for long. Flawless, but of this earth, nevertheless. It too will come to nothing. Jesus teaches, **"For what profit is it to a man if he gains the whole world, and loses his own soul? Or what will a man give in exchange for his soul?"** (Matthew 16:26). Those who have obeyed the Gospel understand our duty to teach. Before His ascension into heaven, Jesus tells His apostles to go into all the world to teach and make disciples (Matthew 28:18-20). The same words apply to Christians today and every generation. In the book of James, he teaches **"Let him know that he who turns a sinner from the error of his way will save a soul from death and cover a multitude of sins"** (James 5:20). Saving a soul from death refers to spiritual death. Souls continue to head to an eternal damnation at their disobedience. We must be compelled to teach of God's love and mercy, yet warn of the assured end for the unbelieving. God clearly gives the facts in His word: **"Behold, all souls are Mine; The soul of the father As well as the soul of the son is Mine; The soul who sins shall die** (Ezekiel 18:4).

God has been clear about the details in the New Testament. Do not think that somehow the Law of Christ is lax and ambiguous. We must give diligence to all scripture. Paul tells Timothy, **"Hold fast the pattern of sound words which you have heard from me, in faith and love which are in Christ Jesus"** (2 Timothy 1:13). That pattern has detail, and we are called to take notice and obey. This is an act of faith and love. God expects us to be attentive and to accomplish all He has sent us to do. If He did not, then Christ's words mean nothing: **"God *is* Spirit, and those who worship Him must worship in spirit and truth"** (John 4:24). We should not disregard scripture to suit our own feelings or think it optional. Believe the scriptures are inspired of God (2 Timothy 3:16). By this faith, we commit ourselves to them.

How do we win souls? Years ago, congregations actively

door knocked to reach people with the Gospel. At the time, it was an effective way to teach. Today most homeowners do not answer the door to a stranger. After a day of work, the garage door opens then quickly closes with no interaction with neighbors. We have become a people of isolation in our comfort zone. Conversing about religious matters is tantamount to giving detail of your latest medical procedure. No one wants to hear. Radio broadcast of religious topics were greatly popular in previous generations but no longer. Sending biblical material through the mail remains somewhat effective, yet most end in the kitchen garbage before reading. Consequently, sharing the Gospel with others today can be difficult, but the command still exists. Family would probably know of your belief so the time to have discussions may come about. Gaining trust in friendships can be another opportunity to let others know what the Bible teaches. Even those we see in daily routines are souls needing the Truth. Handing a tract, card, or church bulletin for someone to read is not hard. Pointing out a streaming service of Bible lessons or giving a DVD to view on their own is simple. Sharing your faith on social media is a way to have others read scriptures or extend an invitation to worship. Many have computers along with the means to connect with people. Even this book I have written has been the catalyst to reach others with the truth of our souls. Times and methods change but the need does not. We must find ways to teach the unbelieving in humility and love.

What do we teach to win a soul? Teach the truth of the Bible which was taught to you. Start with the basics beginning in Genesis with the evidence there is God. You will be shocked how many do not believe that certainty. Because of the education system separating church and state along with the atheistic doctrine layered in many subjects, generations of children have grown without any spiritual foundation. It would be more likely they believe in alien life residing next door than the fact of Creation. Teach the love of God. He sent His Son to minister on earth and be our example, ultimately suffering on the cross to save us from our sins. And it is personal – He died on the cross for my sins. Sin separates the soul from God. A soul in sin cannot go to God but will be cast into damnation. This may sound cruel. This may sound hateful. God's justice is not swayed by how we think or see things. The biblical text brings a realization. God means what He says. If He did not mean what He said, then His laws would be toothless, and His justice a joke. God's justice is set, it is righteous, it is eternal. Our God, who is all powerful, has the final say, as Jesus warns in the book of Matthew: **"And do not fear those who kill the body but cannot kill the soul. But rather fear Him who is able to destroy both soul and body in hell"** (Matthew 10:28). Tell of the steps of salvation in hearing, believing, repenting, confessing and being baptized (immersion in water) to then continue as a faithful follower and servant. Teach the value of *one* as taught in the New Testament: **"There is one body and one Spirit, just as you were called in one hope of your calling; one Lord, one faith, one baptism; one God and Father of all, who is above all, and through all, and in you all"** (Ephesians 4:4-6). This verse refutes the vast number of beliefs, countless denominations, and doctrines of men. The Bible confirms there is only one of each seven words mentioned (body, Spirit, hope, Lord, faith, baptism, God). It matters. Finally, of great importance, teach that the Bible is full of love, joy, and peace, leading to a home with God for all eternity.

> **"For I am persuaded that neither death nor life, nor angels nor principalities nor powers, nor things present nor things to come, nor height nor depth, nor any other created thing, shall be able to separate us from the love of God which is in Christ Jesus our Lord"** (Romans 8:38-39).

It is a book with a lifetime of learning. Take God's commands seriously and His love to heart. It will mean the difference to your eternal life. God uses imagery expressing what awaits in Heaven. Its splendor is revealed to our finite mind in the book of Revelation. But what joy in the words "forever and ever"! Read and re-read the essential words in the Bible to satisfy your soul.

And he showed me a pure river of water of life, clear as crystal, proceeding from the throne of God and of the Lamb (Revelation 22:1).

They shall see His face, and His name shall be on their foreheads. There shall be no night there: They need no lamp nor light of the sun, for the Lord God gives them light. And they shall reign forever and ever (Revelation 22:4-5).

www.ingramcontent.com/pod-product-compliance
Lightning Source LLC
Chambersburg PA
CBHW060949050426
42337CB00052B/2778